# TRACING BODIES

# TRACING BODIES

## VIRGINIA WATTS

OSP

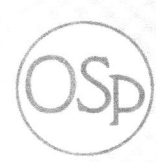

# TRACING BODIES

Published by Old Scratch Press,
an imprint of Current Words Publishing, LLC.
Dianne Pearce, editor and publisher.
David Yurkovich, design.

This is a work of fiction. Any similarities between actual places, events,
or people, either living or deceased, are entirely coincidental.

For permission requests, contact the publisher.

Library of Congress Control Number: 2025934409

ISBN: 978-1-957224-59-6 (paperback)
ISBN: 978-1-957224-53-4 (epub)

Printed in the United States of America.

**FIND US AT**
oldscratchpress.com
currentwords.com

For my writing friends who critique my work.
No one gets very far alone.

# CONTENTS

**TRACING BODIES**

# Snake I

As the story goes
my grandmother's grandfather
was the county jail keeper
small town, deep mountains
ring of clanking keys
volunteers who delivered hot meals

In the jail yard an ancient tree
held up a wood plank swing
where my grandmother played
pushed her doll or pushed it empty
not much of a story until the first gift fell
from a fourth story cell
landed like a bird feather
at a little girl's feet
pencil drawing of a black bear cub
so realistic she kissed it
transfixed by its friendly, shiny eyes

During months that followed there was a beaver
white tailed deer, porcupine, bee, muskrat
mountain lion, peep frog, owl, wolverine
skunk, squirrel, butterfly and oh the snakes!
when my grandmother waved toward sky
mouthed *thank you*
hands would appear to clap
through barred window

She kept the drawings
stacked inside a dressing table drawer
paw steps, flipping tails, night howls
held at bay under a river rock
the serpents were masterpieces
so lifelike we'd gently tap their scales
watch them slither around the page
dart of dark forked tongues that made us squeal

# Snake II

my grandmother Ruth spent her lifetime
in a cabin tucked into Elk Mountain
born and raised there
birthed and raised a family there
heard patterns in falling rain
wandered with stars as her company
cherished the phases of the moon
sensed the presence of wild animals
stayed stone still until they passed

Springs she planted a field of pansies
I see in my dreams. Summers she
stuffed her cabin with bluebells and lilies
Autumns we hiked to the top of Elk Mountain
picnicked within a gem-colored surround
Winters we laughed as wind howled loud
in the chimney pretending to be a ghost

When a snake sunk her fangs into me
Ruth dried my tears and my blood
applied ointment, bandaged my calf
brewed peppermint tea, served warm
molasses cake with whipped cream
on a pretty pink pottery plate. Told me
I'd scared that snake half to death
when I dove into a part of Elk Creek
the snake called home. Just because
a snake bite hurts like the dickens
doesn't mean the snake wanted it to

My grandmother Ruth
spun away her old age years
until one day in early June
sunlight beams radiant
inside a bedroom window
of thick, wavy glass
she didn't open her eyes

# Henry

was a ghost
my cousins and I were sure
who wore tartan sweater vests
even in summer heat as part of his disguise
always in the meetinghouse graveyard
white ponytail and mustache, corncob pipe
back stooped to yank weeds, rake leaves
guide a push mower between rows
straw hat bowed, bobbing

We'd chant *Morning Henry* or *Hallo Henry*
*There's leftover peach pie inside, Henry*
to be polite but mostly to hear the only sound
he uttered – *humph* - not a gruff *humph*
not an annoyed *humph*
more a hum of kind acceptance
whisper of a passing breeze
when he died, we learned his full name

For his many years of volunteer work
Henry was granted a sunny burial plot
nestled near the quiet, shadowy forest
that cradled the meetinghouse grounds
after that we drew hot pink chalk hearts
on a smooth creek rock
left atop Henry Albert Cott's spot
because he always answered

# Ester

On Sunday mornings my grandpa
visited his brother's house
insisted I go too because Aunt Ester liked me
I never saw much of Uncle Ike
bedridden from a coal mining accident
just his feet through an open door
bottom of a mattress, row of tiny tombstones
under grey wool blanket

*Coffee, Ester!*

*Turn up the heat!*

*I need my sweater, Ester!*

Ester was nice, gave me gifts
she scrounged from the house
porcelain teacup, silver thimble
even though my world was Barbies
bubblegum and bikes. I sat alone
in the stifling living room as she
scurried back and forth, huffing
shoulders hunched, armpits wet

*Coffee, Ester!*

*Where are you woman?*

Ike coughed, hacked, ptuied
into a spittoon, an object I never saw either
just heard a clang like a peach pit
shot into a tuba's throat
while over the mantel dewy-eyed Jesus
kept offering me his drippy heart
like a cold drink of water

# Clayton

Clayton was slow our parents said
to us he was nothing but sweet
full of smiles, mostly he played
with plastic trucks in his backyard dirt
but when we walked to The Church
of the Nazarene, Clayton tagged along

We all loved that nearby graveyard
behind a church none of us went to
one gnarled tree, easy to climb
birds calling, butterflies floating
stray cats dozing in the sun
ancient headstones, chiseled
numbers and names we stuffed
with yellow buttercups. We knew
about old age, death, funerals
skeletons, didn't care

Clayton's favorite angel stood atop
Mr. Harvey Tingle's gravestone
Tingle died in 1897. His angel
had massive wings, unfurled
all the way to catch a mighty wind
she stared down at the ground
a real pity, since her home was up

One day Clayton lay on his back
on top of Tingle's plot, squirming
to get a better view when a minister
came outside, told us Clayton
didn't know how to act
that we were no longer welcome

We walked a sobbing Clayton home
his mom saved the day, gave us
ice cream sandwiches. *This town
is full of graveyards and Clayton
now that an angel saw your beautiful face
she'll find you wherever you go*

# Dad I

On the boardwalk, a massive Viking ship ride creaks and groans. Blinks orange and red lights. Rises and falls. Builds momentum like a runaway train. I envision my father among the arm-flailing passengers. All of them about to be hurled into a churning, tempestuous sea. Dad in rain-soaked khaki who hung on to a rope above his bunk in the belly of that ship for dear life. A high school senior who graduated early. Enlisted. Trained to serve as a tail gunner.

The ship captain's voice. *Say your prayers and goodbyes, men. This is a hurricane. Thank you for your honorable service to your country. We stand together. Be brave.* Hang on Dad, I whisper under my breath. You don't know it yet, but you're going to make it.

Dad's body dangles between whippings at the mercy of gale force winds. What if he's shredded to tatters. What if he loses his grip. What if the ship rolls over and dumps a thin boy into pulsing swirl, an endless tunnel drilled through an endless sea.

Countless times, sitting on his knee, I begged him
*Tell me again about the storm and the ship
and how you were sure you weren't going to die*

# Horse

There was this mean horse
we all knew
he was a real mean horse
snorted and stomped
slashed air with tail
tossed head
curled lips
snarled yellow teeth
lowered his head
to face us
brown eyes coppery
on sunny days
pinned wide and frozen
all the whites showing
dead giveaways
real madness there
real mayhem
we scaled grey stones
to stare
entranced by a beast
roped to a stable

That horse finally bit a kid
from another neighborhood
who was probably too chicken
to let go and flop back down
onto hard ground
when he should have
you can't shinny down
an old wall that crumbly
after that the sign went up
NO TRESPASSING
DO NOT CLIMB WALL
we cursed that coward
our bellies straining
from car windows
to capture glimpses
of rump and mane

black tail beating back
back and back
at nothing

# Alice

I forget how I broke
the glass thermometer
my cheeks hot and dry
when I discover
cold silver
an enchanted worm
from Alice's land
to roll across
kitchen linoleum
that breaks
into beaded segments
and puts itself back together again

I pull up my shirt
rub what I've found
and therefore is mine
into the skin of my chest
*finders, keepers*
will fantasy
*drill deep the core of my heart*
so I too can
tumble down a hole
and dwell in a land
of magical beings
with magical mountains
cradling magical metals
where no child
will ever get sick again

# Janitor

Why did we have to memorize that rhyme in elementary school
Thirty days hath September, April, June and November
I mean, there were calendars hanging in every classroom

Why are the leaves that tumble down in the early fall already dry dead
I always want the colored ones to let go all at once like a ticker tape parade
Fill the air with flutter of color and wing

Why did they wait so long to let us use pens in school
Too many years of sharpened Fort Ticonderoga No. 2 Pencils
I mean, where was the confidence

I hope it snows this coming winter because last year not one frosty flake
Nothing that gathered and grew taller in the silent, frozen yard
Nothing I could walk out to and erect a cold person

Why did they have to make Frosty the Snowman weirdly scary in animation
like the janitor in the basement of the school who wheeled a yellow slop bucket
turned around slowly at the sound of my steps, grinned at me like a hungry pumpkin

# Banquo

A dog barks and I return
to an evening from childhood
It's not so much that the sun is gone
or that a lone dog has made himself known
What is special are the two orbs
the sky moon and a ghost moon
who sleeps on the bottom of the bird bath
Poor drowned ghost. No, no, that's not
what I was thinking back then

The ghost moon in the bird bath
floats on a feather raft
Any minute he'll sail into the air
and land inside my cupped palms
He's just tiny and perfect enough to do that

The screen door whines, thuds shut
here comes the steady plod of my father
across backyard grass. He stops at the swing set
folds his arms over his chest, cocks his head
to the side. This makes his grin crooked
The sky moon glints in his teeth

*You gonna swing 'til dawn or what?*
*Can I?*
*No. Time to come inside.*
*But the ghost moon is back in the bird bath*

Dad's head swivels, spots him

*Banquo? Again? What's he want? An audience?*
*I think so*
*Such a showoff. This isn't the Globe*
*I know*
*Think he'll finally fly tonight?*
*I do*
*Fine. See you for breakfast*

# Bully

Our wooden desks
had carved-up tops and dark mouths
where bad kids hid bad things

The worst bully in the class was T
He harbored mean moods, had an older
brother who beat the shit out of him

T stole whatever he felt like from any kid
a birthday doll hurled over playground chain link
toward certain death under the next freight train

One day T pulled a rusted hunting knife
from his desk. I was expecting the usual picture
naked woman ripped from a drugstore magazine

Grinning lightning bolts, he stabbed
the chest of the air, blade tip aimed straight
at me until I nodded, knowing what he wanted

Remember the troll under the bridge? That was T
I blinked at the words chiseled into my desktop
*R.S. 63', Jack T. 1969, Merry Christmas, Fuck you*

When the teacher began spinning planets
in a model of the solar system
she turned her back to the class

I scooped white paste from the jar
inside my desk, raised a brushful
to my mouth and painted my tongue

T's snickers erupted like a million matchheads
struck and tossed on a gasoline road
crisscrossing the dark side of the moon

# Little Sister

Eight years old
sneak to our grey wood barn
old game freezer, treasure trove
for all things
I am too young to hold
sling shots
bow and arrows
a cut and gut fish knife
*That freezer smells*
*like an old man's toe jam*
*STAY OUT OR ELSE!*
my older brothers warn

They can't scare me
I want their guns
orange plastic ring caps
whatever it is
that makes them wild
to kill each other
how they hoot and holler
real smoke galore
endless gasping antics
*You got me!*
bodies that roll down hills
come to rest
in still little piles

One afternoon
they go to a Pirates game
and I rob them blind
shoot up all their ammo
in seconds
Are they mad? Sure, they are
They are *rip roaring* mad
but I don't care
My brothers are big, fat liars
killing turned out to be fun
but not as fun
as they made it look

# Dad II

I watch his lying lips
lips that have always been
on the thin side but now
they are barely there
imploding along with
the rest of him
shoulders unrecognizable
neck so scrawny
I imagine chicken bones
buried there
*No, I didn't fall. I never fall*

That's when an old woman's
bluish hand drops
from white-sheeted gurney
in the corridor a hand
that swings once
before hanging limp
silver charm bracelet
cloudy diamond
pale pink nail polish
hand that gripped monkey bars
a boyfriend's hand
scrubbed parquet floors
changed bawling babies
clapped at dance recitals
gardened
water colored
played parcheesi
pressed the remote
hand like the trembling hands
in church pews
I remember as a child
clinging onto rosary beads
prettier than jeweled necklaces

When the doctor asks me
*Did your Dad fall?*

my father's broad hands
cup his mouth to *boo*
the doctor the same way
he used to put lousy
baseball umpires in their place.
tentative *booing*
answers from another room
then another
the place catches on fire
in the uproar
my father grins like a schoolboy

# Dad III

After Dad died
I kicked myself
Of course, he
prepaid the
cheapest
crematorium
he could find
bunch of con artists
weeks went by
no return calls
when they finally
answered the phone
proclaimed the job complete
I knew it was a lie
a sham in an urn

After that hoodwinking
I researched options for
my someday dead body
maybe human composting
very Green Movement
thirty days, aerated chamber
Dad would have said
that is a ridiculous price
to shell out
to turn a dead body
into a shoebox of soil

Once he attended
the viewing of
an employee's wife
at the wrong
funeral home
bowed his head
over the wrong
dead body
later demonstrated
the bow for me

explained
*It was too late*
*I was already in line*
*The woman had a very*
*pleasant face, made me*
*think of dear Aunt Bee*
*from Mayberry R.F.D.*

# Fish I

When his heart failed him
my dead father remained
seated upright on the toilet
for six hours like the stoic
soldier he was until help arrived
I was not surprised
Dad always tried to make
dreadful things better
sometimes it worked

Sometimes it didn't as in 68'
when the fish tank filter pump
petered out while my family
vacationed. We returned
to a grisly scene, green muck
goldfish afloat. *Have Mercy*
*Try to think of this as something*
*else like Aunt Nancy's horrid lime*
*Jell-O and mandarin orange slices*

I threw up while he carried
the tank outside, dug a hole
but then he grilled hamburgers
*Sure hope Bloomer Weaver*
*doesn't get a whiff of these*
*before we get to eat 'em*
Bloomer Weaver being
the actual name of an actual
man from his boyhood town
a hamburger glutton

Who wouldn't giggle at a character
like that even if I'd heard the story
a million times, even if I still long
to climb inside a Country Squire
fill up at Esso, and return to the land
of sand, seagulls, and horizon
made of nothing but moving water

# Dad IV

When my brother phones
to tell me our father is dead
I see the tattered hole
in my brother's
bedroom window screen
the single shot
he misfired
that didn't kill anything

No small animal
lying still and crooked
in backyard grass
though we went
outside to be sure
as our father requested
from a kitchen chair
where he sat sipping
black coffee reading
The Patriot News

No harsh words
No punishment
No longwinded speech
about how a BB gun
is not a toy
Wag of his head
Cluck of tongue
*Nothing dead then, kiddos?*
*No.* We chimed monotone
*How about some bacon and scrambled eggs?*
*No thanks.* We refused
*Everyone makes mistakes. Have some breakfast*
*No thanks.* We repeated

When my brother phones
to tell me our father is dead
I hear wind whining
through a hole

A sound as high pitched
as a fly stuck
between pane
and screen
I stumble
to a nearby window
and search
for a body

# Pete

Power just went out
No lights in the house
My heart pounds, still
the five-year-old who wailed
if the lamppost went dark
convinced it was the heart
of our house, so Dad
let it burn all night

I need to get a grip. The sun
always rises. Even if I am out
of candles and my flashlight
has taken a flight to the moon
I'm fine as I was seconds ago
iPhone charging, bulbs glowing

If Dad were here he'd tell me
to stop holding my breath
*for Pete's sake,* referring
to the dead mouse we found
in our fireplace one autumn

When the small, grey body
rolled out, I screamed. Dad said
*For Pete's sake! This guy deserves
a proper send off.* Petrified Pete
was so cute in his Kinney's shoebox
near the cheerful, orange blaze
we built, a cotton ball for a pillow

Dad asked Pete's soul some questions.
*Where you from? Tunkhannock?
Lots of lumbering in those parts.
Got a favorite color? I bet you
would look regal in purple. Favorite
cheese? Swiss? Funny, you strike
me as more of a Roquefort man, Pete*

'Twas a fine farewell for our guest.

No longer alone and afraid in the dark

# Aunt

The hilarious part is how we think
Vienna Sausages are exotic
suitable for a silver tray
to be served at an adult cocktail party
skewered on toothpicks
arranged with edible flowers
pinky-sized hors-d'oeuvres from a can
slimy, slathered in sweet tomato sauce
perhaps a traditional recipe from Austria
a place that sounds like a storybook
where people waltz on hillocks
and falling snow waltzes with them
to music, music box music, a tinkling

My cousin and I discover the sausages
in the far back of a kitchen cabinet
my aunt's secret pleasure something she eats
when she isn't starving herself
which was most of the time and as girls
we know better, know she lives hungry
know we shouldn't steal pleasure from her lips
given how my uncle oohs and ahhs
over any woman built like string bean
*Now that's what I'm talking 'bout*
but there is a car in the driveway
and keys on the counter
and we are still young enough
to believe in escape

# Chicken Bride

Afternoon sun baking
freshly laid manure
My new school friend and I
scale pasture fence
leap cow patties smothered
with flies on the way
to her house
No way to drive to it
No mailbox
No front steps
No curtains
Water pump
Outhouse
with a peeling door
Rusty trailer
dumped in a back meadow
usually for men who harvest and leave

Inside, twin sisters
running around
in pink Huggies
No frig
No tv
Lawn chairs for furniture
we sit on a worn rag rug
and share a bucket
of Kentucky Fried Chicken
a treat just for birthdays
my friend whispers. It's not
her birthday or mine
I make sure I eat everything
even the parts I can't chew. Suck on
bones like she does. We wash up
in a Cool Whip container
of cold water in the sink

I brought my Barbie
and some outfits. My friend

is afraid she will rip
the lace wedding gown
her Barbie looks like the one
my cousin Tammy played with
Tammy's married now
I transform this old Barbie
into a beautiful bride
with my gown. One twin
drops her drumstick
snatches the doll
waves her over her head
between greasy fingers
*Cock-a-doodle-doo!*
The mother yells
raising her hand
to slap the little one
Distant tractor
rumbles to life. We play
with naked dolls now
The twins really need
a diaper change. The gown
washed in pump water
dries stiff. At home
my mother's bleach fails
that gown stinks forever

# Mrs. W

Black two-piece suit
piped gold and silver
Cucumber slice eyes
Pink lips, pink toenails
Can of Fresca, ashtray
in shade under a recliner
I can still see Mrs. W
tanning in backyard grass

Neighborhood men lapped her up
Mowing lawn rows
Yanking leaves from gutters
Resealing driveways shiny
Even my own dad couldn't resist
the occasional glance, an ogle
as he scrubbed our birdbath
frequently and thoroughly

Mrs. W wasn't like my mom
She wasn't like any mom
Chain smoker for one thing
Drove her Country Squire fast
Wore miniskirts, skintight jeans
Knotted her summer tops below her bra
exposing flat stomach, bellybutton
But she did have kids – four of them

One day I am washing my bike
Mrs. W is hosing her Squire
White hot pants, bright red bullseye
on her butt, a heart bite of fresh blood
I look both ways, sprint across the street
         *You're bleeding!*
Mrs. W whips around to face me
girl of seven gripping a soapy sponge
         *Get used it*

# Mountain Cousins

and I swam in an elbow
of Loyalsock Creek
when I visited one summer
my thirteenth August
the coffee-and-cream water
dyed my white bikini
brown as a twig. The suit
too skimpy anyway
I didn't want aunts and uncles
to think my suburban life
of concrete pools, tennis courts
umpteen tv stations and malls
had already corrupted me
the next summer I wore
shorts and a Reese's Cup t-shirt

Making braids on towels
spread over creekbank
my cousin Linda poked me
pointed to a tourist
bragging about capturing
a salamander. When he
realized his palms were full
of orange poop he yelped
and dropped the poor creature
our cousin bellies shook
quietly, so the boy didn't notice
unkind edges don't exist
in that land of tumbling stream
smooth pebbles speckled
as bird eggs, some striped
pink, red, and even gold

I daydream of growing up again
where my ancestors founded
Elkland Friends Meetinghouse in 1872
cleared rugged land, farmed
where I was worthy by definition

where no one cared if I dressed like Tiegs
or played tennis like Evert

I tell myself I could have been
one of them anytime I wanted

# Townsfolk

Mr. Memmi kneading dough
inside The Hershey Bakery
Mr. Memmi the first and only man
who got down on one knee for me
to hand me a hot, powdery roll
the size of my palm I placed
against my cold cheek in winter

Pronio's Grocery Store
selling everything under the sun
from sausage to Snowy Bleach
Mr. Pronio with his utility knife
freeing plastic toys attached to products
*She can have the giveaway prize*
he would tell my mother
*No need to buy anything, Mrs. Watts*

Mr. Tulli fitting shoes, humming Sinatra tunes
never asking annoying questions about school
Mr. Cagnoli's flute lessons
accompanied by two Dalmatians
one head for his lap and one for mine
I'd pause and squeak, forget flats, sharps
on my way out, a candy bowl
*Try to remember to practice this week if you can*

Maybe the whole town was inside a bubble
a Five & Dime plastic snow globe
I know the flakes don't fall by themselves
I know you have to shake up the world
to make a small miracle happen but look
Milton Hershey built a whole town
and a boarding school still birthing
one bright future after another
just by selling candy in this world

I don't believe in any god, no blind hope
of any kind but I do believe in something
I was there and I saw it myself

# CAPT. HUBERT WALKER JR.

Sixth grade girl of the 70s
riding a school bus pinching
a nickel-plated POW bracelet
tighter, tighter around her wrist

Not much else she can do
for CAPT. HUBERT WALKER JR.
try really, really hard not to lose him
remember the letters of his name

That rainy morning
the bus smelled of baking bread
CAPT. HUBERT WALKER JR.
could be starving in a cell in Nam

Maybe he is a really big soldier
Maybe his dad was a Marine too
Maybe his dad calls him *Bruiser*
Maybe he can dig his way out

Sherry Eckert gets on the bus, sees the bracelet
*Big Whoop, is that ugly bracelet gonna save him?*
She has a new Flower Power bracelet of daisies
Sherry Eckert was born full of herself

CAPT. HUBERT WALKER JR.
is a real man in real trouble
and anyway, the world has more interesting flowers
than daises and real daisies aren't psychedelic

The girl checked and
rechecked all the lists
CAPT. HUBERT WALKER JR.
didn't make it

At the bottom of a ballerina jewelry box
among smiley pins and mood rings
CAPT. HUBERT WALKER JR.
was put to rest

# Hank

Tagging along with my dad to pay a bill at Hummelstown Fuel Oil, a poster reached out and grabbed me. **Leisure Lanes Youth Bowling Leagues Forming Now!** Dad sought the advice of the ancient guy inside the fuel oil office whose scowling face made me think of a totem pole character. George knew everything about everything. *They don't have pool tables or smoking inside Leisure Lanes, do they George? Nope. Just lanes. All on the up and up, Ralph.* The deal was sealed.

I lived the joy of entering Leisure Lanes nearly every Saturday morning for six years. Dad was the one to drop me off and collect me because my mother couldn't fathom why a girl would want to bowl. Dad always had a parting comment. *Don't eat anything mushy from the vending machine. Don't snack after you stick your fingers in one of those rental balls. Don't throw anything heavier than 12 lbs. Get me a hotdog with yellow mustard and don't tell your mother.*

Once inside Leisure Lanes the real world disappeared. A dim, windowless, banquet sized hall with beautiful, gaudy carpet. Black balls gliding down oiled lanes as if there was no traction, no earthly gravity. After a while the crashing pins sounded like music, crystal goblets toasting, theater applause. I loved the rental shoes damp from the last occupant, scuffed, worn, ill fitting, something I only wore there, the air vent on the ball return that dried my sweaty hand.

There is not much else to do inside a bowling alley except bowl. That's the beauty of it. Ten frames. A finite set of chances. I did collect my share of Wild West charms, super balls and mood rings from the gumball machines and eventually I became a reasonably good bowler. Still, I faced days of gutter ball games and isn't that life.

There is a Staples now where Leisure Lanes used to be. I went there recently. It was an empty feeling place, but I managed a few phantom practice throws in Aisle 5 between the printer cartridges and office trash cans. When an employee approached to see if I needed help, I wanted to ask. Where's Hank?

Hank was the maintenance guy at Leisure Lanes. If your ball got stuck, your lane wouldn't reset its pins, find Hank. He spoke in two-word phrases. *Don't Run. No Shouting. Whose Coat.* After working in the bathroom. *Toilets fixed.* If he had to fiddle with a malfunctioning gumball machine. *Wrong Coin.* If you needed change. *Front Desk.* Heavy snow falling. *Closing early*.

The last Saturday of my last bowling league at Leisure Lanes, Hank was standing by the front doors swilling a Kelly-green bottle of 7-Up. Hank liked 7-Up. And because he knew everyone's parent he glanced at me, pointed to a powder blue 1965 Cutlass idling in the parking lot. *Dad's here.*

# Brother I

I am not going to write a poem
about guns used violently in
nightclubs, theatres, fast food
restaurants and please know
how horrid it is to press
these letters
S – C – H – O – O – L – S.

I am not going to write a poem
about shock and crushing despair
the inane, insane way we debate
more passionately than we
mourn dead
C - H - I - L - D - R - E - N.

I am not going to write a poem
about guns used violently
in schools against children
because it is not my place

I am not a parent who has
had to answer that phone call
I am not a parent who has had
to physically accept remains
I am not a parent who has lost
my whole world in one day

Instead, here is a short entry
about me as a child perched
at a peeling picnic table
outside in afternoon sun
on my maiden visit to a
shooting range

I am licking a cone of
butter pecan ice cream
the only flavor offered
at the snack bar, a flavor

only adults like, spitting
nuts into a paper napkin

The earmuffs my older brother
clamped onto my head are
enormous. They have slid down
to form an ugly necklace
I am jumping like mad
in my seat. Every gunshot
shocks me. Gunshots are
much louder than you expect

I want to enjoy the vanilla
ice cream between the gross nuts
I try repositioning the muffs
over my ears but they fall back
down. I try watching fingers
pulling triggers so I can stop
being so terrified. I focus
on my brother who is kind and
good but he and his fellow
shooters have stepped inside
the same smokey mirror
reflecting robots loading
cocking, lifting, steadying
squinting, aiming, firing
BANG, BANG and BANG!

I have seen shooting before
in technicolor Westerns
with characters named Haas
or Wyatt who are mostly
silly and good at whistling
but this shooting is not that

Head ringing, I trail behind
my brother, not to the paddock
to untie his horse as I wish
but to his dented-up Chevy
parked in a cinder lot of butts
and Pabst Blue Ribbon caps

my hands sticky, a wailing
reverberating inside my ears

# Mary

My purple snow boots punch holes
through the ice-crusted sidewalks
that loop the Catholic church and Parish School
on my way to Daniella Sabatini's tenth birthday party
strolling the side of my hometown
where the families live who built this town
generations who toiled inside a factory
opened a grocery store, shoe shop, restaurants
birthed squalling babies and baptized them
my Protestant mother puzzles over this Catholic majority
gold medals around their necks
a multitude of saints and ceremonies
Daniella's elaborate First Holy Communion dress years ago
worn on one occasion: the day her soul married Jesus Christ

When His mother calls out to me now
it is a female hum in winter wind
I know she stands in the garden
beside the house where the priests live
where nuns clothed to their toes in black
cook, clean and do laundry
no human woman has hair the color of rain-soaked tree bark
scalp that sprouts a perpetual gold and pink crown
dress the robin's spun from spring's blue sky
I see what her problem is
standing on my tiptoes
I brush snow from her mouth
she looks down at me
smiles and whispers
*Run!*

# Turtle

I pity this creature
who drags the world
around on its shoulders
we all think we have at times
but that's crap. A turtle's
burden is so immense
it can barely inch along
can't saunter, stroll, skip
or jump. Turtles often die
stuck on their backs
slow roasted by the sun

A turtle shell isn't even
technically a shell
they can't take it off
like a jacket or coat
this shell is body
spinal cord, ribs, nerves
no shell, no turtle
when the hare lost to the
tortoise, a type of turtle
it didn't want to become
a tortoise instead, trust me.

I watched my cousins butcher
a turtle only once. Hung by
its tail from a clothesline,
the headless creature
could still move. It fought
valiantly against death
I couldn't imagine
it was fighting for life
shrunken elephant feet
kicking back, back at
serrated knives slicing it
closer to freedom while
from a transistor radio
propped on a tapped keg

Lennon sang that above us
there was only sky

# Lassie

The weather where I lived
suddenly turned demonic
I say *where I lived* because
in some part of the world
all hell wasn't breaking loose
people were sipping cocktails
fingers of the sun warm
on their shoulders and thighs

It rained day and night for a week
a constant drumming, torrents
lashing our windows. When the winds
kicked up, the chimney howled
*Noah should be here any millisecond,*
Dad said. *Don't worry, this won't happen again
for a hundred years*

We bailed out our basement
bailed out a neighborhood
of basements, ate what needed
to be kept cold, too much ice cream
watched a parade floating downhill
in the drainage ditch. Lawn chairs
tricycle, clothesline of drowned white
work shirts, basketball, kiddie pool
a whole family of fiberglass lawn deer
and Lassie, the grey poodle who
lived at the top of the street. She in
her hot pink collar ran to the bus stop
every morning to lick my ankles
now, her still body sailed by
riding up and over the current
like a graceful canoe

After that, I stopped drinking
a person can face only so much
fluid. No more water, orange juice
V8, Tab, 7-Up, or limeade for me.

I'd been bugging Dad for years
to let me have a beer like my older
brothers. A few days into my boycott
he cracked open a warm can of Schlitz
handed it to me. *Ten is old enough*

# Suburban Kids

We ran barefoot across lawns
that bled together, a soft, green sea
identical brick ranchers bobbing
boats tied together and anchored

Buried in our sea, sewage tanks
their round, concrete lids tiny islands
we stepped onto, chins high as Armstrong
stepping onto the surface of the moon
*Does anyone smell anything?*
*What if this thing erupts like Vesuvius*

A sewage tank hatch makes
a perfect home base, meeting
place, flat surface for cards
board games, séance candles

Incidentally, they can't be pried
open with six screwdrivers
pushing upward all at once

On July 4th of '73 we met
at my hatch to watch the top
of the town fireworks
being launched miles away
to swap snacks, hopefully candy

Jake hadn't been around
No one wanted to ask why
his birthday hadn't changed
our lives as expected. I lost
Rock-Paper-Scissors-Shoot
I had to ask the questions

*Long time no see, Jake.*
*We heard your parents*
*are getting a divorce.*
        *Yep.*

*Why?*

    *My Dad threw a brick through*
    *our bay window and the puppy*
    *ate some broken glass.*

*Is the puppy okay?*

    *Yep.*

*And that's why they're divorcing?*

    *I guess that's all it takes.*

*No swing set for your birthday now?*

    *Nope.*

*What'd you bring?*

    *Pretzels rods and two sticks of Juicy Fruit.*

*That's it?*

    *Yep.*

*Toss it up*

# Brother II

The first time I discovered the only star
that stays in the same place in night skies
I was in the backyard with my big brother
Mark was humming "Hey Jude"
accompanied by a chorus of crickets

*What's that?* I asked, pointing upward
he stepped away from his new telescope
a birthday gift, to follow my finger

*That's Polaris, a 70-million-year-old star.*
*If you ever go to the North Pole, the North Star*
*will be shining directly over your head like a halo*

*Let's go there together someday.* I said

I told everyone during grade school that Mark
was more brilliant than Einstein and Sagan combined
I told everyone at my 20th high school reunion
he'd been too brilliant for this world and that's why
he let drugs and booze swallow him alive

You can only discover something once
taste sun-warmed watermelon, grip a squirmy fish
lose your stomach in the plummet of a rope swing
believe in an outer space of hope for the future

Now whenever I locate Polaris in dark atmosphere
I tell myself that stars eventually die too and only
a crazy woman would trek all the way to the Arctic Circle
to encircle her head in the flicker of memory

# Brother III

*-    In memory of my brother Mark 1953-2000*

When it is dark on this planet, I examine
images from the James Webb telescope
dissolve into memories of my big brother
I lost decades ago. He would have loved JW
Look away from where you are rooted
I tell myself. Think beyond your life of one

In '72 it felt more like a life of two
Mark and I, armed with paper sky charts
spent hours on backyard grass squinting
at mostly the moon's contoured face, what we
could see best with a mail order telescope
*I bet there's a galaxy beyond our galaxy, beyond*
*the Andromeda Galaxy, where everything*
*is orangey green and works opposite of here*
Mark's response: *You're nuts as usual*

Sometimes in the backyard with him,
the star charts, and the scope, fireworks
launched from a nearby park. When the first one
sailed into dark sky like a tiny, brave rocket ship
it was all I hoped for. Colors that didn't look
like themselves reinvented the ink of night
He asked me once which color was my favorite
*The one I haven't seen yet.* His response: *That's almost not nuts*

# Brother IV

You knew it made me so mad
when you drew a face on your fist
and turned it into a hand puppet
always the Russian spy Boris Badenov
from The Rocky and Bullwinkle Show
Beady eyes, arched brows, slash marks
for his mustache as if there'd been
a serious shaving mishap
your thumb moving up and down
your voice with a thick accent

*Tell zee dentist drill I said hi*

*You actually got a C in gym class? WoeAHH!*

*Thanks for folding zee underwear so purrfectly*

*Ginnee, at Sunday School, draw me a picshore
of Jesus getting into trouble*

You and your stupid Bic pen
I was ten years younger than you
Where was the mercy for a little sister?
You relentless tease. You brat
The whole thing still makes me mad
maybe that's why at the crematorium
when the guy in the same plaid jacket
Rodney Dangerfield wore in Caddyshack
handed me your ashes, I could barely
grasp the urn. *Bless you, Miss,* he chirped
smiling as big as a horse

Padding down carpeted corridor
toward the exit it was all I could do
not to hurl you through a window
my tears came then. Hot as blood
I should have thrown myself at you
when I had the chance. I should have

beaten you silly until you stopped
swallowing all the things that killed you
but then I laughed, laughed until I howled
in the heart of a crematorium
If some grinny guy in a ridiculous jacket
had handed you your urn of ashes
instead of me, you would have said

*What izzz zat, buddy? My carnival prizez?*

# Madge

Madge owned a country store in a tiny mountain village
I liked her. She never yelled at me when I picked up toys
Yo-Yos, cap guns, doctor kits, marbles, baby dolls

She sat beside the register, wore cotton tops
sprinkled with tiny flowers, pansies, yellow roses
smelled of rosewater, never said much to children
which made me like her even more, just
*How are your grandparents doing, Virginia?*

My favorite thing in the store was the glass case
stocked with candy even in winter when no one
in their right mind traveled that far north
except for family. My grandparents lived
in the middle of that dense, shade-laden forest

The day of all days came when I was eight
I'd tagged along to the store with my grandfather
who needed gas for his snowplow from the rusty pumps
I was sent inside to buy a metal tin of Saltine Crackers
five-dollar bill clasped in my hand

As Madge bagged crackers, I admired the glory of candy
inside a glass case. When she snickered, snorted
or something stranger, I dragged my attention away
from Smarties, Jawbreakers, Bazooka

Black licorice hung from the side of Madge's mouth
shaped like Frosty the Snowman's pipe. She handed
me one. Together we shared one hell of a smoke
I can still feel the elation, the naughty freedom
sweet syrup dragged to the mine shafts of our lungs

# Deer

All night snow falls in buckets as if to bury us alive. In the morning, we dig a pathway to the garage, my grandparents and me, and head to Quaker meeting. The wind yowls, rocks our car, a toy boat on a listing sea. Bright white pastures drop away into bright white horizon. I squint at trees that stand alone here and there, shorter than they should be, branches bowed. People who didn't run fast enough to find shelter.

*I feel like we are driving across the moon,* Grandpa says, and we could be, if not for the dead buck slack-jawed on the side of the road. He lies in a bed of startling crimson, cherry syrup that drenched my summertime snow cone. I feel guilty for thinking about something silly.

*Cursed logging truck,* Grandma hisses. It's always a logging truck. The killers careen down narrow mountain roads, overloaded, behind schedule for a delivery to the mill in the low country. Bullets on wheels, we call them.

Grandpa stops, swings open the car door. It whines a mourning for the poor deer. I roll down my window, listen to boot treads crunch across ground pancaked by truck tires mammoth, mighty, and mean.

The animal's back legs are crushed flat. The white-tipped tail is off by itself. Grandpa leans over, grabs front hooves, drags the body into fresh snow. Tan velvet coat, black nose, long eyelashes, acorn brown eyes. When Grandpa stands up, the front of his corduroys are blood kissed.

I sit beside him at meeting with what we could take of the slain life with us. It probably seems like we didn't change anything, that stopping and laying a hand on a dead animal didn't matter.

# Ballerina

The jewelry box ballerina
was clever, turned away
when a machine in China
tried to stamp paint
on her pink, plastic face
didn't want garish red lips
or eyes beady black
I showed her my room
her spot on my dresser top
chipped the paint from her cheek
with my fingernail
nothing could be done
about glued-together legs
arms raised to frame her face

I left her box open, she feared
being locked in a coffin
face down on pink satin
plus who was going to steal
my collection of mood rings
heap of cheap bead chokers
from the gumball machine
at the bowling alley
I never wound the knob
that spun her around
the box played tinny music
and pirouettes made her seasick

A month was all I could take
before I used Dad's wire cutters
to snip the metal spring
that chained her to that box
she was free, her brittle smile
safe inside my palm
the ballerina couldn't dance well
but she could hop
enjoy simple pleasures
float in a boat, glide down a slide

ride inside a Matchbox car
head stuck out the window
slips of fresh air wild in her hair

# Wagoneer

Man, I wait for it, the shoebox-sized covered wagon with the red and white checkerboard awning from the TV commercial to explode from a closed kitchen cabinet and gallop between my mother's bare, blue-veined legs. She's wearing a yellow terrycloth bath robe. Her black hair is fuzzy from another toss and turn night.

I'm daydream-begging for the give and tug of reins. The clippity cloppity of miniature horse hooves across kitchen linoleum. Come on, little Chuck Wagon, show yourself. Let's go. I'm having a conniption here waiting for you.

It doesn't matter that my family doesn't have a dog. I'll give the food you ferry, meaty beef chunks smothered in tasty brown gravy, to our neighbor's grey poodle Mitsy. She's a beggar. Just please, please come to my house with your wagon and your horses. Leap out of your hiding place and scare my mom to death. Make her spatula sail through the air and boomerang back to her open hand like a magic trick.

Skid under the kitchen table. Take a sharp turn and head for the living room. Teeter for a few thrilling seconds on just one side, on just two wheels. My father sits at that table, bent over a cold plate of breakfast eggs trying to convince himself at the start of another day that my older druggie brother isn't headed for the worst of endings.

Make Dad jump in his chair. Knowing him he'll get right into the swing of things and yell out something perfect like *What in tarnation?* And then wagon man head straight for me. I'm here in front of the tube watching *Charlie's Angels* with Malibu Barbie and Ken who are bickering over the one measly beach towel they own to share between them.

I'll shout with sheer joy when you run your little team over my bare feet. Oh, the tickle of hoofs. The glide of wheels. Let me chase you all through the house with a lasso to whip and whine above my braids. Three bedrooms. Bathroom. Basement. Garage. I'll follow you straight through brick and mortar to backyard grass. Does it hurt to travel through a solid? You disappear into wood and sacks of dog food all the time, so I'm not really worried about it. We can vanish from this neighborhood like a pinprick of light that winks once on the edge of a vision.

We'll go wherever you want to go, Chuck Wagon. You and I can find every hungry dog that lies on the edge of all the worn-out braided rugs in all of this world cuz if that's what you want then dag gummit that's what we'll do. Ya! Ya! Giddy Up!

# Snake III

My cousin Lina and I dangle forest miracles from our fingertips. Delicate ghosts that sway back and forth in spring breezes. In these mountains, snake skins are common as stones, sticks, and dirt. Perfectly intact from snout to rattle. Lighter than paper, finer than our grandmother's Parisian scarves.

We shouldn't mess with the skins. They deserve better than our grubby hands, the piles we make as if they are trash to be burned.

Usually left out in the open, we discover one tucked deep underneath the fading white blooms of mountain laurel.

*Leave that alone.* I blurt. Lina backs away. *What's eating you?*

What if the snake is nearby. Watching us. Coal eyes shiny with tears. Forked tongue stabbing air for the first, delicious, raw scent of someone she is missing. What if she left her skin so that he would be able to find her.

What if he is wandering. What if none of us know when we are lost.

I gather branches, tuck them around my skin as camouflage.

My voice trills through tree boughs, descends as lilac mist overtop fieldstones near the lake.

My fingertip sculpts a single ripple that rushes through nightfall to a faraway shore.

*Here I am. Here I am...*

# Classmate

The girl stank
maybe her family
rationed fuel oil, hot water
Family of six boys and this girl
living in a cabin in the woods
behind the abandoned boy scout camp

What was her name?
Mandy? Francie?
Tall, boney
Hair ragged
as if she cut it herself
Baggy t-shirts
Knock off Keds

She rode a rusted Schwinn
I'd seen before
at the bottom
of the town dump
where my brother
shot BBs at trash

In middle school
embarrassing things
began to happen
I worried
What if the girl
couldn't afford
feminine sanitary products

What about the dispensers
in the school bathrooms
If she'd asked
I would have given her
one of Dad's screwdrivers
for keeps. I guess she managed

# Mother

has forgotten about the sun
her gaze gauzy, living room window
bay shape she has always detested
*Here comes the mailman*

My father is in the Rehab Center
our king and conqueror
of transient ischemic attacks
*Your father's strokes are just mini strokes*

Stacked in a corner of oil-stained garage
forest green plastic lawn chairs
unparted for cobwebbed eons
*Virginia, what are you doing out there?*

On the small concrete front porch
of that one bath, three-bedroom rancher
I place two empty chairs in the sunshine
blinded white spiders skitter up and down the legs

*Come outside, mother, it's so nice*
*Those yellow flowers by the lamppost are pretty*
*What are they?*
My mother's mouth is a fist

When we were little truant kids
my older brother would make his fist talk
by moving his thumb up and down
*You're in big trouble*
*Mom says you have to go to bed early. Sucker!*

My mother lifts her eyes out of the fathoms
*Those flowers?*
*They came here on their own*
*I don't know why*

# Sunbathers

The town of Hershey
is tearing down
the old Plaza Pool
I park along Cocoa Avenue
trail clover to chain link
they're gutting her, alright
bet she's tough
been here since 1966
still, they've plucked
her diving platforms
scraped her belly
clean of tiles
now she's white
not ocean blue
the deep end
felt deeper
than it looks now

A slide remains
one of those plastic tubes
the original, open air one
was better
polished silver
hot as flame midday
fast as lightning
a real straight shooter
a fight for your life
all the way down

Concrete steps
still hanging on
spine crushers
where my best friend and I
smoothed our beach towels
white bikinis
beaded chokers
Bain de Soleil
oranging-up our skin

gingerbread
lingering on taste buds
another shared
Big Town Pie
whiffs of chlorine
mixing with chocolate
from the factory
two blocks away

Voices falling, rising
children laughing, crying
punches of shrill whistles
"Walk! No Running!"
my brother's transistor radio
propped between our heads
Casey Kasem's
Top 40 Countdown
Fleetwood Mac
*Go Your Own Way*
The Bee Gees
*How Deep is Your Love*
Starland Vocal Band
*Afternoon Delight*

We were juicing our lives
looking for looks
sure, we should have been at the library
reading *The Sound and the Fury*
for English class in September
scooping applesauce
at the old folks home
but this was our time
to be conceited and thin
to lay our bones out on display
to knock 'em dead
rough concrete under our feet
sting of treated water in our eyes

# Daredevils

Friendship forged in AP science classes
him, gentle-hearted genius
comfortable in the contours
of his own brilliant mind
Both fans of TV's The Addams Family
grim, tuxedoed butler Lurch
who answered the mansion door
At the sound of the class bell
we mimicked him...*You rang?*
I was a bus student. He drove to school
Often arrived late with an excuse
*long train on the tracks today*
In our small-town, train tracks
were spinal column

On the way
to summer jobs
football stadium
*Rumble Rumble*

Across the tracks
to the library
community pool
grocery store
*Rumble Rumble*

Crisscrossing
for the dentist
7-Eleven gas pumps
*Rumble Rumble*

Night of high school graduation
my friend and his gang of loveable
concave-chested boys were sure
they'd calculated to the last
second the time needed
to drive their station wagon
off          the          tracks

Crossbuck flashing red
Conductor's piercing horn

# Server I

The skin on our server's face, perfectly pale
black bullet suspended from a silver chain
swings forward, falls back, against boney neck
that diminutive missile his only eye contact
young man seems hunted, no haunted
dogged by a hopeless dream
bad peer group, the bully called regret

I hurry our table along ordering dinner
to allow the teenage boy to escape
restaurant's porch incubator hot
crimson light from a wall heater dyes
grey shadows of his sleeve tattoo apricot
pulses black lines raven purple

When the child sets down my glass of Prosecco
as gently as an embryo clasped between the tips
of silver tweezers I whisper, *I like your arm art*
pale green irises meet mine, a smile dawns
he caresses creation, lowers the forearm to me
points to roses of all sizes and shapes
some in bloom, some buds, others crying petals
*My mother wants to get a tattoo just like mine now*

# Server II

The server at Denny's, as beautiful as Diana Ross, is fed up
she's slamming down diner plates, silverware
her sneer says shut up or get out and who could
blame her. The place is a dump. Even her false
eyelashes are ungluing themselves to escape
sticky tables, ripped seat cushions, crummy
carpet, toddlers screaming, customers bitching
about cold, 45-minute late eggs, coffee rings
inside mugs. Are all Denny's in Georgia shit?

The server's name is Georgia too as the regulars
know, including the toothless, young woman
wearing a rumpled Mickey Mouse sweatshirt
who carries an infant in a car seat to a booth
unbuckles it, rocks it, hugs it tight to her breast
coos to the naked body stiff as death, a plastic
baby doll wearing knitted booties. Georgia
pretends to heat the pink bottle the woman
yanks from her diaper bag by disappearing
into a crashing, hollering kitchen, re-emerges
to test the formula's temperature, three drops
of air on her delicate wrist, before she hands
the bottle back. *Here, Momma. All ready now*

# Server III

She'd been beautiful once
that, anyone could tell
even now
willowy legs
flat stomach
fine boned
pale green eyes
transcendent
despite the bags
the smoker lines
etched into her face

She waves men in biker jackets
to freshly wiped tables
a Waffle House near Daytona
where cooks shout orders
sausage, eggs barely over
grits, wheat toast done dark
she floats her smile
through rows of filled chairs
coffee pot in hand
like a torch that lights up
her own asphalt road

It's the way
she smiles at the men
their broad chests
heavy boots
deep voices
smelling of sweat
worn leather
open road
the way she scribbles food orders
in a leopard print notepad
bending down
to look them in the eye
like a teenaged
lip-glossed
halter-topped

Tinker Bell

It's the way
she lays checks down
pauses sometimes
when a man
has the same bend in his nose
a similar chortle laugh
how her knuckles
stroke shoulder blades
back and forth
linger there
in dappled shade
of a creek bank
secluded
save the riot
of birds chanting in time
with a pair
of runaway hearts

It's about
who he was
to her
then
what she believed
she'd always be
to him
how hot
his skin was
how sweet
his mouth
like grapes
gone soft
how it hurt some
and just enough
how afterwards
her fingers shook
underwater
when they dove in
to swim

# Mourner

I wander rows, sprays of spruce, bows
plots adorned with grave blankets
as if bones can be kept warm
once they are on their own

In the distance across field and river
the buildings of Manhattan
cold and grey as these monuments
winged angels, boxy mausoleums

I assume the man is here
to visit his wife, he's brought her
a poinsettia, shiny green foil
decorates the pot, white price tag
stuck on clear plastic around petals

His foot is perched on its rim
three times wind snatched the poinsettia
tumbled it away from him
the man's wobbly legs gave chase
trapped the object like a soccer ball

What will he do? Cast around for a stone
to weigh down the pot, take it home
to his undecorated apartment in Queens
throw it away, fall to his knees and dig?

A swarm of squawking crows
unfolds and folds upon itself
a giant, pleated, ebony fan settles
on nearby tree branches, refuses to quiet

Birds take flight, a wild, rolling wave
black specks careen into a blue future
the man lifts his foot, the poinsettia tilts
wind wins, strews the red of her
across trampled terrain a dazzling stain

# Neighbor

Every morning the front door
swings opens and he appears
stooped man clad in green robe
slippers, white ash ankles
hair unkempt he closes
the mammoth entryway
leans his arthritic back
against its panels before shuffling
across the street to his flock

He tosses wheat toast he detests
from linty pockets
to geese that wobble
from a lapping lake
to pluck, squawk and hiss
at the man who owns the dock
gigantic beach mansion
crumbling drive, dated Mercedes
blanketed by autumn leaves

Every morning his mother
stood before the blue flame altar
of a gas stove, peach velour robe
hair set high in curlers
insisting between drags
of a Benson & Hedges
that Wonder Bread was pure crap
her copper teapot whistling
the end of something

# JT

In Lenox, Massachusetts
I searched for James Taylor
He lives there. Somewhere
I have captured flecks of fire
and spatters of rain
since the age of thirteen
just to show him
and I am dying to know
if I can become a moonlight lady
I think I have potential
I'm a day dreamer after dark
with a multitude of song lyrics
locked in my heart

But James wasn't downtown
in the Get Lit bookstore
No Sweet Baby James
in the pub on Main Street
where I nibbled olives
feta cheese and crusty bread
careful to keep my lip gloss intact
The bartender said he hadn't
seen him around either
so I ordered more wine

My last stop in Lenox
was the Gulf station
on the outskirts of town
where rusty mobile homes
turned the snow pink
I felt better there
on the A-side of the state
land of deep pastures
dotted by bird feet, animal paw
where the Berkshires
kiss the chins of clouds
hum something soft and kind
an album on a Zenith stereo system
spinning round and round

# Forrester

Outside the world is about to burst into flames
grass sickly yellow, flowers face down
trees seem shorter, as if bending the knee to our sun
I swear that orb looks twice as big as ever
been toying with us for many a millennia now
always had the power to roast us alive if it wanted to
we're at its whim and it's either fresh out of mercy
or hates the living guts out of earth's every living thing

I venture outside and gasp in the driveway
birds and bugs silent, no flicker of squirrel tail
on the porch next door Forrester the hound
doesn't lift his lug bolt of a head like he usually does
I wave anyway and he summons a burst of life blood
thump, thumps his tail in response, such a good boy
doesn't do much, won't chase sticks or bark at strangers
mostly lopes around his yard chewing rocks, stinking to high heaven
but I always pet him and whisper in his ear *I love you, doggie*
I bet I've done that thousands of times, so you know,
if we all burn up in this heat wave, I think I've done okay here

# Cardiologist

My cardiologist wonders aloud why my ascending aorta dilated so dangerously. He calls me *his* patient and that makes me feel special. *I'm glad we caught your condition in time for preventative surgery. Otherwise, I would have heard that my patient died in an ER somewhere.* I don't know what to say to that. What would he have done if I had died suddenly. Remembered how cooperative I was? A few of my better jokes? I imagine him receiving the news. *Really? Shame. She was asymptomatic and what a hoot.*

Sometimes I want to bear hug this stranger I've known for a decade and a half and feel him squeeze me back. I want to ask if he prefers tuna fish or egg salad for lunch. Does he worry about nuclear war, dementia? Has he ever been drunk as a skunk and if so, where was he, and how would he rate that experience? Do he and his wife whisper in movie theaters? When his father died, did a little piece of his heart shatter? But the visit ends with a cold handed handshake, a predictable *keep up the good work*.

Walking to the EXIT I resist spinning around to wave like a kid on a carousel of painted horses. I won't see him for another year. I wonder what he'll do during the in-between. 365 days of bedtimes, garbage days, sneezes, novel plots. What will be his favorite part? The first snow fall, the magical kind that sifts down like talcum powder, a call out of the blue from an old college roommate, a warm, soft sweater, gifted to him for his birthday, a rainstorm that leaves behind a land of mirrors.

# Surgeon

When the surgeon said
*this is an aorta at risk*
for a split second
I thought he was talking
about something else
a bike tire, family business
our democracy
I concentrated on his hands
so I wouldn't
blubber like a baby

His hands were small
talcum powder pale
fine of finger
he held them limp
while he explained
that if I opened my heart to him
my chances for a full recovery
were excellent
what he really meant was
I had no choice
unlike John Ritter who was a hoot
starring in Three's Company
what guy wouldn't want to reside
with two cute chicks

In the end I had to use
my own trembling hand
to sign consent forms
which meant I resigned myself
into the hands
of someone I'd just met
with a reputation for being excellent
with his hands
I've never been good at faith
faith is blind
but at the end of the appointment
I reached for a hand
and it was given

# Baby I

I am drawn
to manhole covers
ancient, cast-iron ones
gates on the ground
to keep people
from falling down holes

Brilliant idea except
what lies at the bottom
haunts me
a hiss perched atop
the crooked spine of the wind
*Come over here*
*Look down*
*I dare you*

I try very hard not to
terrified of the evil, sinister acts
men can do
1971 newspaper article
scorched into my memory
partially decomposed
baby
spied in a storm drain
city of Harrisburg

I see her there
tiny fists
swaddled torso
the filthy cloth
her eyes
focused on the sun
passing in millimeters
over the grates

# Baby II

I lost Jesus
for three weeks among the chaos
of moving boxes
found him again
cradled in the arms
of my son's baseball bobble heads
who agreed with everything he said
which was nothing
my Jesus is plastic
glossy peach
pinky-sized
part of a Woolworths nativity set
displayed every Christmas
because the idea
of an adoring, forgiving,
selfless, eternal little lord
is ridiculously intoxicating

I despaired the loss of my babe's
empty golden manger too
the rounded indentation
where his cute, little butt would lie
curly head
chubby arms open wide
how he wanted me with such fervor
the temptation of his red cherub kiss
at times low on hope, sad on life
I'd grip his hard, little fingers
gaze into those baby blues
this infant so awfully cute
so totally dope
I could almost hear him
babble and coo
but I know my heart
wretched thing chides me
*Don't be an idiot*
*You know you can't believe*
*in a love that pure - Jesus Pure*
*No matter how many times it is offered*

# Mothers

The young mothers
are tired
they exchange
children's ages
potty training tips
good nursery schools
babysitter contacts
on their iPhones
*I'd give anything*
*for a full night of sleep*

I don't tell her
how pointless
eight hours of sleep
feels at sixty
that someday
she will ignore
house repairs
tinkling toilet
drippy faucet
loose gutter
just to hear
something
when she awakens
in a stone quiet dark

One young mother
is taking the class
while her son
is at daycare
to lose
her baby fat
I don't tell her
how useless
the fat
I carry around
on my hips
feels with no one

to prop there
how there is
no one
to pick up
and drive home
that I never make
funny faces
in my rear view
anymore

One young mother
misses a clean house
and breakfast out
I don't tell her
how much I try
to enjoy hot
unforgotten coffee
how last evening
I was down
on my hands and knees
scrubbing
a spotless kitchen floor
where my daughter
lost a lavender
Polly Pocket high heel
during July of 2002
that when
my hands were dry
I didn't
go outside
to catch lightning bugs

# Sports Fan

Man in an orange jacket
crooked mouth, droopy eye
one leg withered and weak
swings his foot wide
then plops it step by step
as he climbs to his seat
high in the clouds
above center ice

He's a big man
tree trunk torso no one
will be able to stop
should he lose his grip
and tumble down
steep rows toward
the frozen white oval
where young bucks
strong as grizzlies
fly fast as fire

Every now and then
he pauses
yanks up his pants
glances back
at battling sticks
the plastic cup of Coke
in his free hand
weeps like a wound
healing itself

Eyes fixed on the next
concrete step ahead
he smiles now
straw clenched sideways
between his teeth
its paper wrapper
dissolving in his mouth
the taste of something
bitter but pure

# Friends

Now that I am 60 friends are ominous
*Downsize now. Sell your house*
*Decide where you want to ride it out*
*No stairs. It's a one level life for you*
*Sort out those Medicare options pronto*

My hair is thinner, teeth less tight
A flatline waits for me and still
I don't listen, haunt my favorite bars instead
Sip Prosecco on ice. Order yummy shit food
Fried chicken sliders. Potato skins. Nachos.
Bask in the glow of overweight off-key bands
who perform billboard hits of the 70s and 80s

What are some of my favorites?
*Best of My Love*
Corny, romantic, heart swelling
Lyrics like that undead me
*Our House* births my truest smile
Cozy room, cats (2) mew, frolic of fire
*Summer Breeze's* screen door slaps a kiss
Window curtains breathe jasmine in, out

Why not ride it out humming inside
a sticky wooden world, wobbly stools
laminated menus, tilt of tap, chink of glass
neon lights to flash in teeth like the sun's
teasy wink in a sideview and voices
yours and mine, all of humankind
the gentle drone of pollinating bees
sudden laughter to sting the eardrum
with the miracle of a grazing bullet

# Fish II

We moved to a townhouse
after thirty-two years
in a 4-bedroom colonial
2 kids, 3 cats, 1 dog
a snake once that somehow
found her way to our foyer
family of raccoons nested in the attic
and one day I got so sick
of cleaning the ick in the fish tank
I flushed its last two inhabitants
down the powder room bowl
where they swam up again
scared the bejesus out of my husband
resulting in an incurable guilt trip to this day

I asked the junk men we summoned
What do you haul away the most?
Foul mattresses? Rusty metal filing cabinets?
Sour smelling Orientals? Little league trophies?
Singer sewing machines? Barbie Dream Houses?
Styrofoam gravestones for Halloween? Dart Boards?
No, they said, bean bag chairs, oodles of them

All those warm, hairy arms
the perfumed wrists
boney backs
with the strength of a bear
all those hugs
oodles of them
we held onto
clung to
closed our eyes to
and forgot
to remember

# Artificial Intelligence

AI doesn't scare me
even housed inside
new lifelike robots
A robot's skin
will always be cold

AI can't appreciate
what fresh cut grass
smells like on a hot
buzzy July afternoon

AI won't cherish
moos of a cow herd
the funny way flies
swarm their tails

AI will never savor
the warmth of a lap cat
gentle toll of distant bell
smell of home
when you open the front door
after a long, wearying journey

It goes without saying
AI can't experience
spinning intoxication
of falling in love
can't desire anything
certainly not the shudder
of orgasm, the clutch of sheet

AI will not dig deep
find willpower to push
a baby through to light
cradle the slimy miracle
in imperfect, freckled arms

AI lacks all concept

of what it feels like to be sick
anxious, terrified of war
injured, betrayed
disillusioned, alone

And how about the loss
of my friend's son
to a fentanyl overdose
AI possesses no soul
who boneless, collapses
so that it may heal
in a quiet, static river

Human souls
restore themselves
crawl forward
on their hands and knees
already my friend can taste
her morning coffee again
and last night she texted
an emoji of a full moon

I rushed outside
as neighborhood windows
glowed golden with family
the moon was with me
impossibly perfect
and skittering across horizon
freeway of car lights
such a beautiful howl

# Bird

A tiny bird
clearly frantic
clearly dying of something
on the edge of my driveway
excess heat, cancer, fertilizer pellets
old age, it's hard to tell a young bird
from an old one

I considered capturing it,
ferrying it to a nearby vet
or swaddling the thrashing body
inside one of my kid's old baby blankets
holding it tight until it settled down
to go easy into what it didn't need to be
so terrified of

In the end, I did nothing
No attempt to halt flops and rolls
hush hissy gasps, left the bird alone
to get the job done, returned later
to glossy black wings
limp and still
wispy grey bugs
scurrying eyelids
twig legs curled
toward an indigo belly
still round with breakfast

I gave thought to a shovel
a shoe box, eulogy
peace in the great beyond
but what was the point
the story of dying was over
I covered the bird with moss
left her where she'd fallen
a shame she panicked the way she had
because look at you now
still as stone
as willing as river current

# Acknowledgments

Grateful acknowledgments to these publications where versions of the following poems first appeared:

*Atticus Review* : Bird
*Bear Paw Arts Journal:* Brother III
*Cloudbank*: Ballerina
*Eclectica Magazine:* Aunt I, Wagoneer
*Evening Street News:* Dad III
*From the Depths Literary Journal:* Mary
*Levee Magazine:* Horse
*Neologism Poetry Review:* Mourner
*One Art Poetry:* Friends
*Poetry Quarterly:* Sunbathers
*Rising Phoenix Press:* Surgeon
*SLAB:* Server III, JT
*Slipstream Magazine:* Deer
*Streetlight Magazine:* Mother
*The Banyan Review:* Classmate
*The Share Journal:* Snake II, Brother I, Mothers
*Two Hawks Quarterly:* Dad IV, Brother IV
*The Write Launch:* Mrs. W, Townsfolk
*Words and Whispers:* Clayton

# About the Author

Virginia Watts is the author of poetry and stories. Her work can be found in *The MacGuffin, Epiphany, CRAFT, Tne Florida Review, Reed Magazine, Pithead Chapel, Eclectica Magazine* among other publications. Watts is a four-time Pushcart nominee. Her debut short story collection, *Echoes from* the *Hocker House* (Devil's Party Press) was a category finalist in the 2024 Eric Hoffer Book Awards, selected as one of the Best Indie Books of 2023 by Kirkus Book Reviews, and won third place in the 2024 Feathered Quill Book Awards.

More at virginiawatts.com

Discover a different side of Virgina Watts
in the award-winning literary collection,

# ECHOES FROM THE HOCKER HOUSE.

"Entrancing, edgy, and melodramatic"
**KIRKUS**

"Outstanding"
**MIDWEST**

"Highly recommended!"
**READER VIEWS**

- 2024 CATEGORY FINALIST, ERIC HOFFER BOOK AWARDS
- 2024 DA VINCI EYE FINALIST
- 2024 FEATHERED QUILL BOOK AWARD WINNER (BRONZE)
- 2023 KIRKUS BEST INDIE BOOKS OF THE YEAR
- 2023 NATIONAL BOOK AWARD NOMINEE

Available in paperback, eBook, and audiobook formats from
Amazon, Audible, B&N, and other retail outlets.

Oldscratchpress.com

www.ingramcontent.com/pod-product-compliance
Lightning Source LLC
Chambersburg PA
CBHW071104120626
46546CB00003B/1272